EVERYTHING

IS

BRIGHTLY

BURNING

CRYSTAL ELIZABETH WESTMAN

Copyright © 2024
All rights reserved.
Published by Sanderson Books
ISBN: 978-1-0690034-0-9

Shh, come quick. Here's a match to strike the saddest day. Let us kerosene the night—and watch together as it all goes up in smoke. Let the cinder set as it should, and may we not worry all that much—when everything on earth is brightly burning, everything, including you.

– Crystal Elizabeth Westman

TABLE OF CONTENTS

Pg.6 AUTHOR NOTE

Pg.7 ACKNOWLEDGMENT

Pg.9 INTRODUCTION

Pg.15 JUST VISITING

Pg.19 IT'S OKAY

Pg.21 WALKING BACKWARDS

Pg.25 TEARS FALL UPON A DYING DAY

Pg.29 HEARTBROKEN ANIMAL

Pg.34 THE DAY THE SUN FORGOT TO RISE

Pg.40 LOVE YOU NOT

Pg.46 SHORT STORY: THE OLDEST DAY

Pg.53 MY FOREST: MY SHADOW

Pg.56 WALKNG FOR WATER

Pg.61 MY BROTHEL: MY WHORE

Pg.64 MOTHER NOT: FEED HIM TO THE CROWS

Pg.70 NINE MONTHS AND A GOD COMPLEX
Pg.72 KARMIC LOVE BATTLE
Pg.75 MARRIED IN MY SLEEP
Pg.80 MEN WALK ME DOWN ROADS I SHALL NOT FOLLOW
Pg.83 EXIT STRATEGY
Pg.86 NOTHING IS LOST
Pg.90 GOODBYE

AUTHOR NOTE

The pecking order is cruel. Yet here we are standing in line.

ACKNOWLEDGMENT

With the utmost respect and appreciation for all human beings, who are just trying to exist, I'd like to acknowledge just how complicated it can be to simply be alive. It would be inaccurate to say we are living in more difficult times than before; it would be incorrect to say life was simpler way back when. Life has always been a mixed bag, filled with good and bad and its peculiarities. This romanticization of the past is a result of having way too much time on our hands to contemplate, and as such, we fantasize of days gone by, of yesteryear, of times we truly know nothing about. Yet, we still struggle in ways humans always have. We cannot ever truly know what it would have been like to live in a different era. We are here now, and that should be enough. To that end, I'd like to say thank you for being here. May we all enjoy it while it lasts.

INTRODUCTION

I once believed the main goal of living was acceptance. Now, further into writing this, I have come to realize, and believe it is simply not true. Acceptance is only part of the equation. Acceptance of a dismal reality, means to be complacent, compliant, and apathetic. And that couldn't be more boring or depressing, to not care about anything whatsoever. There is always something to be done. Even if it is only from our little corner of the world, from within our homes, from within ourselves, from wherever you may find yourself, while the world collapses around us — there is always something we can do to pass the time, to make it more manageable, and worthwhile.

To accept the world as it is, ain't easy, it takes great strength to see the world in its ugliest form, and then turn around and choose to keep on living in it.

If we have no other choice, no other option, and we find ourselves stuck. We shall then turn to our thoughts, and try our damndest to fill our minds with something beautiful.

To resign ourselves is to simply give up.

Let us not falter.

Humans have always found a way. And we will continue to forge ahead with the same bravery and determination as always.

I am not alone when I say I am angry. If there is any more befitting word for how I have felt, it would be—enraged, annnoyed, irritated, upset, bereft, irate and downright despondent (in being placed on planet Earth). In other words, not very pleased at all.

But this will not stop me from trying, and it will not leave me without hope. It will not force me into resignation, nor make me fearful of what's to come. Whatever shall come, will come. And whatever will be, will be. I can learn to accept but I will not allow it to destroy my life. We shall speak out against this feeling of complacency that has swept over us. Let us rage!

Keep going. Keep creating. Keep learning. Keep hoping. Keep dreaming. Keep living. You are worthy of being here. You are allowed to be alive, the same way a plant is alive, the way the dinosaurs once were – the way air lingers – all simply just because.

JUST VISITING

Oh, what a thing it is to be here. To be invited to a place we know barely anything about. Earth—an invitation to live, without knowing the reason why or as to how.

We are allowed to be discontent from time to time. For no one has told us where we are going, and that's enough reason to worry.

So, if you must go, then leave knowing that you've tried.

Do not worry about losing, for nothing here has been lost – just some skin, a little bone, maybe a memory or two.

Don't worry about winning, there was never anything to have won – no trophy for being, no blue ribbon for breathing best.

Your departure may be sudden, and will surely leave many with a mark. But who am I to tell you not to go.

You are not a prisoner, and this is not a jail. Earth is a place to visit, a home to be shared with all, many alike and not so much. Together, we live here, just as confused as the other.

So, if you must, go quietly out the back as to not disturb the others.

Don't forget to leave a clearing—a path for those who wish to carry on the trail you've set ablaze—one made so bright we cannot forget you—a parting gift, if only to remind us you were here.

IT'S OKAY

While everyone is someplace between trying to move forward and trying to forget, there is a rip, a tear in the hearts of many as I write this.

It's okay to be upset about the state of the world. It's okay to be frightened by the future. The world is not as it once was – and may never be the same again. This is called grief, my child. It's okay, let yourself mourn. Let yourself feel. So that maybe someday, not so far away, you may allow yourself to be happy again.

WALKING BACKWARDS

I am currently taking a walk.

I'd be lying if I said it didn't feel like you ripped my heart out and served it to me

I'd be lying if I said I wasn't hurt and saddened by our trajectory

I'd be lying If I said I didn't miss you

I never did care much for lying

The cold has now set in but still find myself taking walks along the pier — frost glazes its surface

We never know why we decide to take a walk or why we decide to end one when we do

How come we don't appreciate walks more? Maybe we would if we knew we'd never take that path again

How we rely solely on our memory to recall every
Stop
Turn
Broken branch
Dead-end

How we think staying on course means taking the same path over and over again

Though along the same path,
Do the leaves not change?
Do the roads not need repair?
Will the cold not turn to warmth?

Because as much as I'm enjoying these walks. I've realized I've never changed course, not ever, not even once

Yet, every day I still take a walk. The same walk – hoping today will be the day the frost disappears

TEARS FALL UPON A DYING DAY

The world is broken and there's nothing we can do.

Even a church pew has its limits before the knees give out.

Why is the earth called round, but not a circle.

Seasons repeat on a rinse cycle.

Where is the center of the universe – did you bring a map?

Shh, do you hear footsteps?

You walk towards the edge of the earth and fall off.

It's okay, falling is just floating backwards.

If it weren't for gravity, you'd fly.

If given a second chance, you'd have jumped - and you know it.

Bring a mop to dry these tears.

Bring water to wash them away.

You'd drink from the ocean if you could, but saltwater wasn't made for drinking.

Yet still you thirst.

And still you weep.

A single shred of hope is offered…

Always right before

you

hit

the

ground.

HEARTBROKEN ANIMAL

If cows were tiny enough to fit in our homes - would we still serve them for dinner?

Or would we love them the way a man loves his wife—well trained

Would we love them more if they came in teeny teacup sizes that fit in our purses

Or would we round em all up and toss em in a blender, the way my girlfriend's make a really good shake

Would our hearts burst open if we knew they had feelings

Or maybe we'd treat them better if we knew they could talk

The way an anglophone treats a foreigner, demanding the whole world speak English

Would we fall at their hooves and repent

If we finally realized humans are not the only beings breathing

That trees can hold a vibration longer than a man's thrust

That a woman's love aches from her innate knowing

A moth gets stuck in a web, the way a man fucks someone he calls lover, other times friend

Salting the wounds of a person, the way you would a really good steak

Another robber breaks in, the way a mortician rummages through the body, always looking for everything you've got

Autopsy complete - we can all go home now — a child waits 13 years to be adopted

A tree chopped down finds itself the same way the gun meets the prisoner in a war

Ten seconds later a bomb drops, but fails to explode, the same way a woman cums – always last

Tiny cows on the porch

                A sunset in the morning

The ocean is empty

                And a baby is crying to be held.

THE DAY THE SUN FORGOT TO RISE

Ah, the sun, isn't it beautiful. It's easy to take something for granted, especially when it's always around. That said, there seems to be an unwritten pact between nature and man, where we seem to believe no matter how terrible the day, or how badly we treat this planet, the sun will still rise, and all will be well.

This unwavering constant has seemingly led us all into a state of denial, a delusion which permeates society and defies all logic. It simply goes against a natural sense of self preservation. This is where we live; it is our home. So, then, why wouldn't we want to take better care of it.

We then deny, ignore, and push aside all responsibility, continuing to buy into the belief that there's nothing to be done. No matter how much garbage we dump into the ocean, or how many cars we drive into a clouded haze — there can't be enough toxins to hurt her — Mother Nature is tough.

I will agree that much.

That is, until the sun forgets to rise — one day bleeds into the next — and we're all left in the dark wondering what happened.

This place we all momentarily call home, this land we leave to our children. Where will they go when the sun is long forgotten?

Will there be enough candles to light their way?

I guess we'll just hang little plastic neon suns in their windows — I'm sure they'll never know the difference.

Science will then create artificial illumination — so that when the day comes, when the sun no longer rises, they will surely give themselves a pay raise and call it progress.

LOVE YOU NOT

I don't love you

but it's not my fault.

A darkened room on a sunlit morning is

still too dark to see

The good is gone, I've folded it up and

tucked it away in the back closet

where nobody can find it

I can't hear you over his breathing

Too many legs around my waste.

I've crawled down this hallway before.

A labyrinth of hands on my breasts

Fingers inside me

But I feel nothing

If you ride a rollercoaster a hundred times, I'm told the drop doesn't really phase you.

Ghosts can't scare you.

Your hands are his hands

Your mouth his own

His eyes the shade of yesterday's shame

I've heard this story before

Yet every time I hear it
I get closer to walking away...

From him approaching me
in the back alley.

That stranger who followed me into a hotel and wrestled me to the ground.

That young guy who climbed onto the roof and broke into my room.

The man who took me in and gave me a warm place to stay.

I wake up to his arms wrapped around me...

14 years old

Cabinet full of coke

A 45-year-old man

A stolen car and my dignity.

My roommate's late on rent again, maybe this time I'll let it slide.

The perfume 'what's his name'
bought me.

The ring my first love gave me,
I always wondered where it went.

I lost it one day on my way to work...
came home to an empty apartment.

Dirty floors.

A darkened room.

And he was gone.

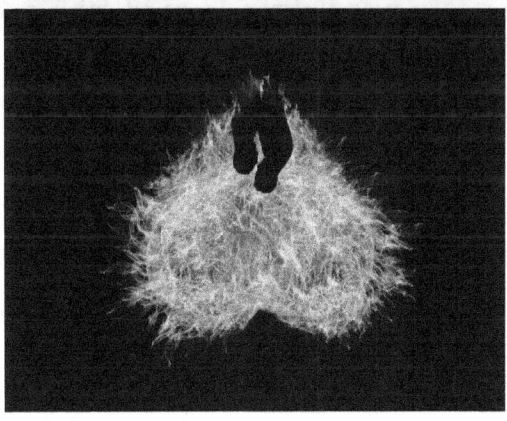

SHORT STORY:
THE OLDEST DAY

You spoke to me as the crow does to the sky, cawing your way into my life the way the cat meets the claw, agreed upon without a notary and a stamp. The lease was written in good faith and a drop of blood, which was my first mistake – but not final.

I looked up at this murder in flight, a flock of warnings circling my life—but I did not run—better still, I stayed.

Entranced, it took me as I watched where the apple hits the ground on an autumn's day.

A blistering of potential, bruised to the core, I did not flinch.

I stood there and waited for them to leave the way the body does the night.

Yet still nothing.

They circled around my thoughts some more.

I looked at my wrist for the time
I had forgotten to measure by age.

My watch was clearly broken.

I then pondered it's reason for being and asked -- why are you even here?

It's hands pointed out to the horizon — but I saw nothing.

I wondered still.

I did not move an inch for hope, the way pagans wait *not* for Jesus.

There must be a better excuse for being than this.

The air brushed past me trying to get
my attention, but still I did not feel it,
still I did not budge.

I tried counting backwards for a while,
then forgot all the numbers and gave
up.

My mind foggy, like the mist hitting the
car window - the lady pulled over to
meet me where I was.

"Choose faster or else," she advised,
her wheels spinning in reverse where
the lines on the map fade out.

There I stood, and there I stayed,
wishing for the answer.

I was at a loss for time.

My skin wrinkled into cloth never worn.

These bones, broken branches on the awning.

My heart a hammer forcing the rusted nail.

My eyes the photographs left behind me.

Then the crows formed a *vee,* and it was done.

A pile of ash on the sidewalk before the cigarette goes out – I turn to dust and disappear.

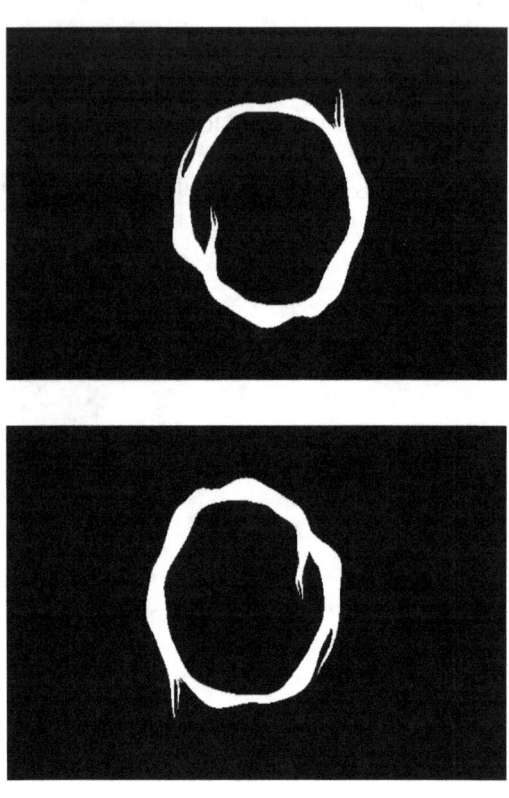

MY FOREST: MY SHADOW

He is a speck in a line of trees, a shade camouflaged into a painting well studied, redundant but preserved by time, the leaves all look the same.

He waits for me there – but will not find me.

My forest is filled with light bouncing off shadow, an iridescent disco spinning

The colors so blinding, a sightless man could feel it

It sends a mother with a needle to her arm into a tailspin.
It takes homeless men to bed and sucks them off

It blankets the bodies sunk in a lake, and swallows the pills of the dying

It throws lavish parties for the hungry, and feeds them a stream of endless fish

Under the bridge, all the men learn to walk on water, while all the good girls sit and clap. Where they're taught to wash the feet of men that don't deserve them—here, they call it love.

WALKING FOR WATER

The car alarm goes off, the sound of monotony shakes me awake.

Neighbors are spinning wheels around the block, every dog's barking for their freedom.

The water station's blocks away and I haven't slept a wink.

Yesterday's coffee and cockroaches in the kitchen.

Refrigerator's still broken.

But the palm trees look peaceful, well rested.

The sky is bluer than my mood.

I gather the used water bottles up and put them in the same grocery bag I use every morning, when I go looking for water and walk.

Let's see, how many bottles do I need? I say counting.

The water money sits on the counter.

The most valued stash in the home.

Count water for blessings, you do not need a well.

The tap runs dry, but around here, you've found true wealth.

No one on the news that you know.

No one banging at your door.

A walk to the water station costs all of ten minutes.

Time is precious, they say, but we all pay for convenience.

Around here, I walk for water.

Around here, they call it life.

The cap twists off, I take a sip, and say thank you

MY BROTHEL: MY WHORE

If brothels serviced women...
Ladies would finally smile, and the war would end.

He moans loudly on a stage

Hardened by ego

He strokes himself to meet her gaze

In the back room, women are being licked for quarters

The music loud enough to hide their shame

Their husbands are home cooking with

the children, all waiting for their moms

to return

Drunken but not angry

                                        Lazy but happy

MOTHER NOT: FEED HIM TO THE CROWS

She said, "maybe."

Maybe I don't want to.
Maybe it's far too much to ask.

After watching her own mother raise a convicted felon, he who was proud of the way he almost killed another man.

Psychopaths are born everyday, she said. After all, they all call somebody somewhere mother.

She was afraid of how she herself felt threatened if she went back to the police. They came once already, but her lawyer told her to lie.

What goes on in your home is no one's business. No one out there is gonna save you. Nobody cares what happens as long it's not happening to them.

And perhaps, maybe they were right.

She thought, if she allowed herself to give life to another, would they be just like her, or worse, just like him?

A poison runs deep in the veins.

It's best not to flip a coin, no one wins playing slots with a rigged machine.

If it's a boy, she could despise him to act as badly as men do, the way society permits them to.

If it were a girl, she might worry sick to protect her from men just like him.

Even worse, exhaust herself to protect them from women—who don't understand—who turn a blind eye and pretend not to notice—the ones who spoil men, no matter how rotten.

Those who compensate for the lack of love they never had, daughters without fathers.

Boys will be boys. They say, what else can we do—lock them up—throw them away with the key?

To that she just says—maybe

Feed. Him. To. The. Crows

Take some accountability

The wound runs as deep as the world's problems, to feel there is nothing just here.

So, when you ask her if she wants to.

She just says maybe it's too much…

maybe

Maybe

Maybe

NINE MONTHS AND A GOD COMPLEX

We are all born of the womb. It takes only nine months to get here.

Only nine months and a day of bloodcurdling screams, flesh and bone, ripped wide open and left for dead — some never make it.

That's what it is to be a sacrificial lamb to the slaughter.

While he, the man, could be any, waits for his legacy to arrive, no sooner than yesterday, to live on in his name.

KARMIC LOVE BATTLE

He's lost himself in the illusion again. He believes himself to be in love, when proof of it is nowhere to be found.

A soldier in a warzone loves his country, too, so much so, he'd allow his body to be dragged through blood, trench, and soil

There is no love there. No respect. No honor. The government and its people do not care. About him, at least, they do not care.

Rather, they'd see him return home in one piece – alive, alive, alive and well—enough to need no one, good enough to love another–strong enough to love himself.

MARRIED IN MY SLEEP

One day you'll wake up.
And have plans every holiday, and the world will call you loved.

You walk towards some flowers and smell the scent of belonging, in a world that hates you - she who is alone but not lonely

Committed to something but not sure who. The road to freedom is paved with men you've tried to love but did not master.

You failed to like them just enough to take you down a path uncertain - where a fantasy meets your only reason

Existing on oxygen alone won't save you.

Your dog can't hug you forever.

When you're sick, who will take care of him?

Who will make you feel normal on a weekend?

The contract is there to bind you

It doesn't care how much you spend

But look how beautiful you now look in the eyes of others, and that's really all that matters

In that dress - worn for only a moment and a day

Worth every penny of sadness.

Let them all eat cake

How else will you eat in a world that wants you to starve for your children.

What else will you do in a world that
wants you kept inside the house
bored.

How else will the floors get cleaned and
the clothing washed, and the dishes
done.

Who will love you now that you will not
serve them.

Where will you go now in a world that
abandons those who love themselves.

PEACE IS THE TIME BETWEEN TWO WARS

MEN WALK ME DOWN ROADS
I SHALL NOT FOLLOW

They tell me to trust them then get lost on the way.

They ask me to follow then demand I carry their load

They want me to believe them then lie to my face

They ask me to praise them when their acts are unholy

They beg me to hear them, but they do not listen themselves

They ask me to wait until they never come back

Never bet on a horse running away from the finish line

Never follow a man down a road if he's not holding a map

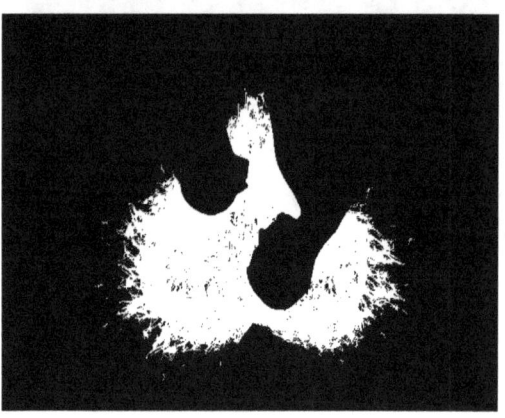

EXIT STRATEGY

There is a door at the end of the hall
that will lead to your next life - where
every choice you've ever made is
pinned against you, a weighted match.

Open the door and walk through.

Wait, the exit sign could be a trick,
flickering in front of the dancing ladies,
trading skin for dollars.

Don't let it fool you, it's the winning
numbers to the ticket you just bought.

Walk through.

Careful, not so fast.

It might be a trap.

Rat poison undetected can kill you. An exit strategy without a plan could, too.

Your next choice hangs in the balance.

Glasses are clinking, men are waiting with their wallets out.

Old lady in the back with her tits out

Boss is late on the paycheck again

They're playing that same damn song.

The alarm system goes off and you win
a prize called freedom

Walk through.

The hallway is long but no longer than
your ambition

The fear will scare you, like the ballet
giving lap dances for a dollar

There will be a single second right
before you get there

It will be then you will finally know
what it means to win

Walk through

Walk through

Walk through

NOTHING IS LOST

Nothing is lost

In an infinite universe

Nothing is lost here

Not even your keys

Everything is somewhere

In pieces

Broken, altered, transformed, worn out

Blt by blt, plece by piece

You, too, can be found

Nothing is lost here

Not even you

GOODBYE

I don't know how to say it, not in

Mayan, nor English.

I don't know hwo to tell you what feels

impossible to say

There arent enough words

To ask you to

STOP.

STAY.

STAND STILL.

DO NOT FLINCH.

Let us take a picture

Make this last

How to stop the world from spinning

Or

The clock from ticking

The clock from ticking

The clock from ticking

WHEN SOMEONE LEAVES, THEY'RE EITHER BUSY WASTING TIME OR WORKING. IT IS NOT YOUR JOB TO TELL THEM WHICH ONE IT IS

HOW DO WE END A WALK?
THE SAME WAY WE END A SENTENCE -
PUT A PERIOD AT THE END AND CALL IT
A DAY

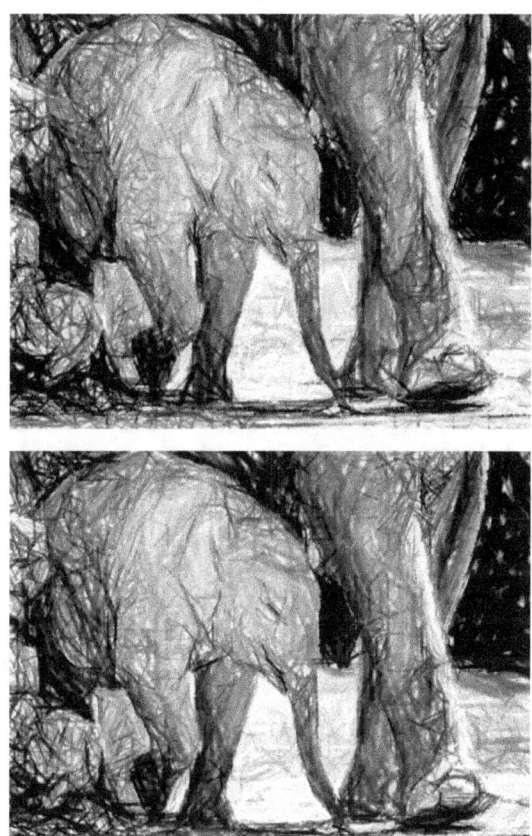

THE WORLD IS BURNING

AND

YOU'RE HOLDING THE MATCH

TOPSY TURVY WORLD

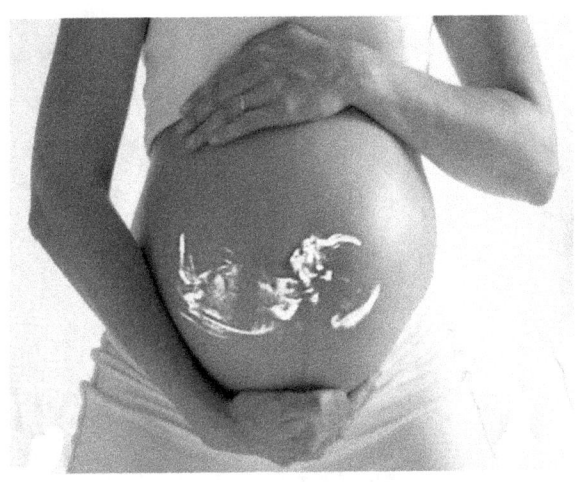
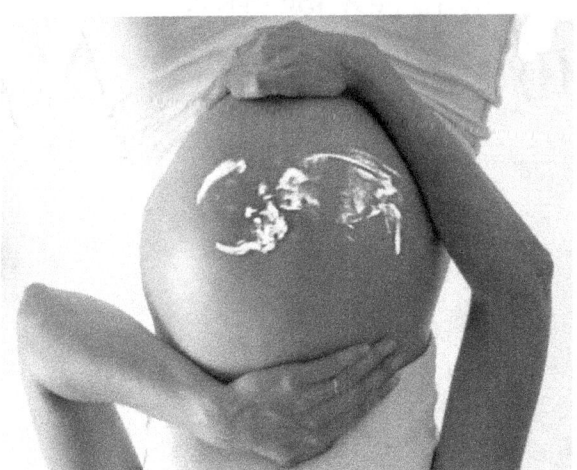

Everything is Brightly Burning | Crystal Elizabeth Westman

WHY ARE YOUR GENES SO SPECIAL?

I'LL LOVE YOU

IF

YOU BUY ME A PLACE TO LIVE

WALK ME TO MY DOOR

THEN ASK ME TO PAY FOR

DINNER

PAY ME A MILLION DOLLARS

AND

I WILL

VOTE FOR YOU

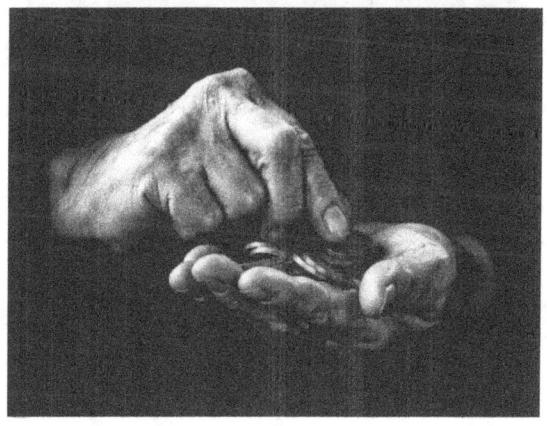

KILL ANOTHER MAN IN WAR – THEY CALL YOU A HERO

KILL A SEED IN YOUR OWN VESSEL – THEY CALL YOU A WOMAN

KILL A FLY JUST BECAUSE – THEY CALL YOU HUMAN

Everything is Brightly Burning | Crystal Elizabeth Westman

ALL THE RICH ARE

ADDICTED TO PLEASURE.

THE POOR ARE ADDICTED TO PAIN.

Everything is Brightly Burning | Crystal Elizabeth Westman

EVERYONE'S ADDICTED TO SOMETHING

THE LONG-AWAITED DREAM

HAS ARRIVED

Everything is Brightly Burning | Crystal Elizabeth Westman

Write me a poem about life

Everything is Brightly Burning | Crystal Elizabeth Westman

Write me a poem about death

Everything is Brightly Burning | Crystal Elizabeth Westman

Write me a poem about the saddest day

Everything is Brightly Burning | Crystal Elizabeth Westman

Everything is Brightly Burning | Crystal Elizabeth Westman

Write me a poem about the longest of nights

Everything is Brightly Burning | Crystal Elizabeth Westman

Everything is Brightly Burning | Crystal Elizabeth Westman

ARTISTS

Angelegea

NietjuhArt

Baggeb

Frantisek_Krejci

Anaterate

Sithuarkaryangon

Shafman

Geralt

Front and Back Cover by Crystal Elizabeth Westman

Thank you for coming.

It's been a pleasure having you.

I hope you come again soon.

www.ingramcontent.com/pod-product-compliance
Lightning Source LLC
Chambersburg PA
CBHW070431010526
44118CB00014B/2002